MW00906086

Frugal Travel Guy Handbook

Rick Ingersoll

Frugal Travel Guy Handbook

All rights reserved
Copyright © 2010
Rick Ingersoll

All rights reserved, including the right to reproduce this book or portions thereof in any form whatsoever, without written permission in writting from the publisher or author.

Published in the U.S.A.

ISBN 1453661530
EAN- 9781453661536

FrugalTravelGuy.com

Table of Contents

DEDICATION

There can only be one "Katybug". She is my bride, partner, best friend and editor of this project. Like the Tammy Wynnette song says:

"Stand by Your Man"

She has done so for years, and I am eternally grateful.

Foreword

Budapest, Hungary 2010

Katy and I are here on a *free* 3 week European vacation with stays in Budapest, Prague, Berlin and Krakow. *Free* business class tickets, *free* hotels, *free* lounge access for breakfast and snacks. All *free* from the tips and tricks I'm about to teach you.

I'm sitting in the Executive Lounge of the Budapest Hilton and so excited to start this project. The advent of the "Amazon Kindle Digital Text Platform" has made publishing this book possible. I read about "ebook publishing" in a Wall Street Journal article last night here in the lounge.

This book is not an impulsive decision. I've been waiting for the right platform for quite some time now. The last time I remember being this excited was 3 years ago when I read a USA Today article about blogging.

The FrugalTravelGuy.com blog has been named one of the "most influential travel blogs on the Internet" with over 1 million hits and climbing. I hope this format is as helpful, and demonstrates that:

"You Can See the World at Prices We All Can Afford "

Katy & Rick
Angkor Wat - Siem Reap, Cambodia

Introduction

I'll never forget the day or place. Mode's Bum Steer, my favorite watering hole in Traverse City, Michigan.

I watched as a guy paid his bar tab with a US Bank Northwest Airlines Visa card. It was 1993. When I inquired further about the card, he said I'd get one airline mile for every $ I spent. I was hooked and yet so naïve. In my experience a good night of dinner and drinks would set me back about $225. It was 225 miles to Chicago. Hot Damn. I had hit the motherlode. Little did I know it took 20,000 airline miles in those days for a roundtrip ticket.

So much has unfolded in the last decade plus. I soon learned it would take more than one night in the bar to get my free roundtrip ticket.

Along the way, we have traveled to Iceland for $64 round trip, stayed at the luxurious La Quinta Resort and Spa in Palm Springs for $40 per night, experienced Europe, Central America and Hawaii numerous times for under $200 roundtrip. We have secured two Around the World Itineraries in Business Class with all our hotels nights free as we saw the sights along the way. Our history of other free trips with frequent flyer miles, it would fill a book just reliving them all.

Simply stated, my goal is to bring you up to speed with the techniques and tricks I take advantage of including the places I look, and secrets I've learned along the way. This pursuit of frugal travel is not rocket science. Anyone can play the game, and take it as seriously as they like. For me, it seems the more I learn, the easier it gets. I hope the same happens for you.

My Definition of Frugal Travel

The main components of frugal travel are typically transportation and lodging. That is where I concentrate most of my efforts in this text. But I certainly will clip a coupon for a discount on a meal, or remember a promotion code for a discount on a rental car or train ticket.

My object is to travel in relative comfort and safety to the places in the world I want to see at the best price I can find.

I'm not a sleeping bag and hostel traveler, although that mode suits many just fine. I'm looking for air travel over long distances and hotels with hot water, no bugs, clean sheets and towels, with air conditioning or heat that works.

If the local non-franchised "no tell motel" is a category 1 and the Waldorf Astoria a category 5, I'm a category 3 kinda guy. Although 5 star hotels are great treats, a clean Courtyard by Marriott, Hampton Inn by Hilton, or Four Points by Sheraton is just fine with me.

In airline travel because of my size and creaky old bones I look for premium economy or first class seating on domestic flights. If not in first class, an exit row seat is a nice catch. On flights across the Atlantic or Pacific I prefer business or first class seats. But I have sat in the cheap seats as well, if the fare was right and the deal outstanding.

The more time you spend on the road, the sooner you'll find a comfort level that works for you. And with that as a goal of sorts, you can decide how you want to fly and what kind of accommodations you require. The only *correct* answer is what best suits you and your travel budget.

Chiang Rai, Thailand

Fare Wars

The airline industry is an extremely competitive business. In addition to this heavy competition, they face a unique situation as once a flight leaves with an empty seat, the opportunity to recover that lost income is gone forever.

At present there are five major airlines in the US domestic market: American, Delta, United (with the Continental merger), US Airways and Southwest Airlines. All are fighting for the huge domestic market. At times the ladies and gents sitting in the revenue management divisions of these monsters decide to tweak their fares in order to "one up" the competition. Let me give you an example in the lucrative Hawaii market.

Delta Airlines has hubs in Atlanta, Salt Lake City, Cincinnati and New York City. American has hubs in Dallas and Chicago. Delta may decide to go after American at one of American's hubs by offering an extremely low fare ($200 round trip) from Dallas to Honolulu on Delta Airlines. Why would they do that? Maybe American has opened up a new route in another strong Delta market in the southeast and is stealing what Delta once thought was their captive audience. Delta has decided to get even with American, even if it costs them money at their small operation in Dallas.

In many instances, American will retaliate by offering a low fare to Honolulu from a Delta hub like Atlanta. The war has begun. Other airlines may join in the fracas, and we, the consumers are the big winners.

Delta may start offering the low fare from United's DC hub, then United drops its fare from Salt Lake City (major Delta hub) to Hawaii. US Airways enters the fray by discounting fares from Chicago and both American and United drop the fares from Charlotte (a US Airways hub) to Honolulu.

This madness can go on for days or sometimes just hours, until the revenue management teams realize they are just hurting themselves. At times I think they are acting like little children and in this instance, I like little kids.

In recent years Katy and I have come to love going to Hawaii; mostly because of the destination but partly because it is a frequent target for fare wars. Here are a few examples of prices we've paid:

$200 including taxes round trip from Newark
$152 and $282 including taxes round trip from Atlanta
$141 including taxes round trip and 2 night's hotel from San Francisco

Note: these trips were from hubs Newark (Continental), Atlanta (Delta) and San Francisco (United). We flew United from Newark, United from Atlanta and the old Northwest Airlines from San Francisco all because of these fare wars.

These prices represent savings of 50% to 75% off typical airfares.

So how do you find these fares and what do you do when you do find one?

Online websites offer you the opportunity to set up and sign up to receive fare alerts for certain destinations when prices make dramatic drops. Some of these sites are Airfarewatchdog.com, Farecompare.com, Travelocity.com, Orbitz.com, Expedia.com, Smartertravel.com and don't forget the airline website alert systems as well. Set the alerts from all the major airline hubs to Honolulu as this is the most prevalent city for fare wars.

In addition, many of the travel blogs online will give you a heads up when a fare war is going on. Whenever I see a fare war to Hawaii, I post it on my blog FrugalTravelGuy.com.

So you don't live in an airline hub city? That's easy. Through the techniques we'll teach you here, you can use one of those free frequent flyer tickets you've accumulated to get to the city of origin of the fare war. Fly free to the cheap fare and you still have a cheap fare to Hawaii. I always keep a supply of airline miles from more than one airline available to fly me to the "fare war" city.

When do you book your fare war ticket? That depends on you. When you first see the fare war, the questions to answer are: is the city of origin located nearby or in a city you can get to by car, train or frequent flyer ticket at a reasonable cost? Is it on an airline you *want* to fly? Or, do you want to wait to see if the fare war spreads to your favorite airline?

Waiting may cost you, or may make your trip more convenient and even more beneficial if it is on your favorite airline. Remember that tickets you buy during fare wars earn frequent flyer miles. It is about 10,000 miles round trip from the east coast to Hawaii and that addition to your favorite frequent flyer account can be significant.

My position has always been when it makes sense: Act Quickly. Nothing feels worse than missing a fare war because I was looking for a little more convenient itinerary on my favorite airline. Remember you are going to Hawaii for around $200.

I'm using Hawaii as an example because it seems to happen so often in this market. But there are other instances of fare wars. One mover and shaker in the industry is the low cost carrier Southwest Airlines. When Southwest enters a new market they often drop fares to unrealistic prices to gain market share. The competitors will match those fares in most instances and retaliate by lowering a fare or two in another Southwest market. It is not just Southwest, but the "Southwest Effect" is legendary in airline pricing. Any airline that offers a fare that is ultimately unsustainable in a given market is enticing a fare war.

Be ready to act quickly and save vastly on a dream vacation destination.

Mistake Fares

This is one of my favorite travel secrets as the savings are huge, the adrenalin rush is fast and furious, and you never know when one will show up. They happen for both airfares and hotel rates. Imagine some new hire, bored employee sitting in front of a computer screen all day entering data.

LGA to DEN $200 base fare, $12.62 airport tax, $.89 recovery fee, $4.36 security fee, M-Th only, roundtrip only, season January 4 to May 8, with exception of May 1, 2 and 3.

Imagine them doing this hour after hour, day after day, week after week, etc. Mistakes will be made and the resulting mistake fares will end up being offered to the public. Airlines publish literally hundreds of fares between city pairs every day. The odds of mistakes happening are very high and I'm amazed more don't surface, but when they do, good things can happen for you.

When a mistake fare or incorrect hotel rate is published, the vendor offering the fare or rate has two choices; honor the mistake fare or refuse to honor the error. In all cases the vendor runs the show and I will go along with their decision. In many cases, in the name of good public relations, the vendor will honor the fare and chalk it up to the cost of doing business.

I like when that happens, and I give them future business as well for honoring their mistake. Really it is no different than a mismarked item in a grocery store, just bigger numbers.

I'm not going to judge your moral position on taking advantage of a mistake fare. Every one of us has to make his or her own decision, just as the vendor has to make his decision to honor the fare or not.

Here are some notable Mistake Fares

British Airways $20 +tax US to Europe
San Jose to Paris $27.88
Chicago to Puerto Vallarta $150 in biz
Watertown, NY to anywhere in the US
for $1.86+ tax.
Los Angeles to Fiji $51
Calgary to Spain $130
Toronto to Bucharest $235 Canadian
Atlanta to Honolulu $152.50
Atlanta to Acapulco $0.00 + taxes
Charlotte to Barbados $28 + taxes
West Coast to Hawaii with 2 nights hotel
for $141 total
Baltimore to Iceland $64 round trip

And here are a few examples of Hotel Mistake Rates

La Quinta Resort and Spa $40 per night
Tokyo Hilton £1
W Hotel in NYC for $20 per night
Phuket Thailand Holiday Inn .01 Bahts
Portland Maine Sheraton $19 per night
Amerisuites Charlotte $1 per night

The Tokyo Hilton mistake was picked by some kids on college campuses and spread around the internet so fast that every Hilton in Japan was booked for the entire summer at the mistake rate. Obviously neither Hilton nor Travelocity could swallow that big a hit so they gave all of us that had reservations a $100 travel voucher for a future booking on Travelocity.

There are many more examples. But from these you can see the huge savings involved in finding and participating in a mistake fare. Some of our most memorable vacations were the result of these mistakes. How can you pass up these rates?

The mistakes all seem to fall in three categories.

"Dancing Decimal" A Business class fare to New Zealand was loaded as $1,438.08 instead of $14,380.80.

"Currency Conversion Error" The Conrad Bangkok Hotel Presidential Suite went for 1935 Thai Bahts instead of the correct rate of $1935 US dollars per night. People paid only $51 for the 2300 sq ft suite per night.

"Forgot a Fare Component" Cheaptickets loaded the fare to Iceland, but forgot the actual fare. They just loaded the taxes and surcharges. We flew for $64 round trip.

you find a mistake fare it really
what type it is. What is important
ly the info you have available about

Act Quickly

These fares can disappear in minutes. Not all mistake fares are honored so do NOT make other travel arrangements immediately. Give the vendor the opportunity to decide if they will be honoring the fare or not. And if not, what type of compensation they may give you instead of honoring the fare. Other people are trying to make their bookings at the same time. Minutes matter.

Your trip should be within all the mistake fare ground rules. i.e. dates of travel, starting city, fare class, class of service, minimum stays, booking agent and routings. No exceptions.

Read everything you can online about the mistake fare *before* attempting a booking.

DO NOT call the Airline or Hotel for clarification until the deal is **DEAD**. Preferably never call. Ask other travelers or knowledgeable friends questions by phone, instant message or email Before You Book.

You'll hear about Fare Mistakes from the same websites that post about Fare Wars, but these last typically a very, very short time. Look for fares mistakes at the airline websites, Airfarewatchdog.com, Farecompare.com, Expedia.com, Travelocity.com, Orbitz.com and Yapta.com.

There is a forum on Flyertalk.com called the *Mileage Run forum* that lists really good fares and is a place to find mistake fares. But as the Flyertalk network grows and more rookies make the mistake of calling the vendor while the fare is still available, the less likely it is that a mistake fare will be published.

My blog and others will post the fares that last a while. Try Frugaltravelguy.com.

The more people that get involved in a mistake fare the faster it seem to disappear. Having a network of likeminded friends certainly helps. Two set of eyes is better than one and the bigger network you have the better your chances of finding a mistake fare before it disappears. Sometimes they last only minutes.

"Our Weekend with General Eisenhower"

The La Quinta Resort and Spa mistake was available on Priceline.com and lasted for several days if I recall. It lasted long enough for me to make one booking of three nights for two rooms and then to return for another one night stay as I realized the deal was worth staying 4 nights.

Some fool went so far as to book over 40 long weekends at the $40 per night rate. His arrogance and greed forced La Quinta to agree to honor one booking only per individual so my extra day attempt was turned down. The lady from the resort that called me was extremely pleasant and professional and confided in me that some had taken the mistake to mean the resort was to become their weekend home for the year.

I agreed with her that excess was out of line. I don't know if she noted my file as a "nice guy" or not, but we got a pleasant surprise upon arrival at the resort.

At check in we were given the Eisenhower Presidential cabin where the President supposedly stayed when he was in Palm Springs for one of his many golfing trips. It all made sense to me when we entered the cabin (villa, suite, really cool pad). The dining room table sat 12, the living room was big enough for a small conference and each room was filled with Eisenhower memorabilia. Our friends were in an adjoining room that must have served as a servant's quarters at some time, but was now elegantly appointed as well. We had a private pool for our use during the long weekend.

I was quite comfortable with the portrait of Ike overlooking the four post bed we slept in. Katy complained of a poor night's sleep with Ike staring down at her. At the time we supported different political parties.

That mistake rate and upgrade was a real treat for us. At $40 per night, we lived the life of Presidential splendor.

"Dumpster Diving for Wendy's Cups"

Late in 2005 Wendy's restaurants teamed up with Airtran Airways for a promotion that had people diving in dumpsters. On each Wendy's drink cup was a coupon good for .25 credit with Airtran Airways. 4 drink cups equaled one credit. 32 drink cups earned a one way ticket and 64 drink cups earned a round trip ticket anywhere in the USA. A 20 ounce drink was about $1.15 in 2005 so for about $70 you could earn a round trip ticket.

Good Old American Ingenuity took over and the frequent flyer crowd went to work. Katy and I heard about the promo just before leaving Columbia, South Carolina for the 3 hour trip to Hilton Head Island. We stopped at every Wendy's on the way — the promo was new and we wanted to cash in on the maximum of 128 credits each as soon as possible.

When we found a Wendy's, Katy would go in first as she is the better looking one of us, and buy a 20 ounce Coke product, asking as she cashed out if she could have 6 or so free empty cups. As I said the promo was new, the staff could care less, and she would return with a handful of cups. I'd then head into the restaurant and try to get a different counter person to wait on me. I'd use the same technique and score a handful for myself.

We repeated this at 5 or 6 Wendy's along our route and gathered quite a stash of cups by the time we hit the island.

Once on the island we'd visit our local Wendy's every day. The "word" got out on what was up and we were limited to only *full cups* at *full* price.

Near the end of the promotion Wendy's drink cups coupons could be bought on Ebay for about $1 each, with the coupon clipped off the cup and washed as well. With a few from Ebay our total take on the deal was the full 256 cups and 4 round trip tickets anywhere in the US. We never added up our out-of-pocket expense, but with that first day haul of freebies, we had very little invested.

I personally swear that I never dove below the dumpster rim for an empty drink cup, but many a collector was tempted. And I'm willing to bet some enterprising Wendy's employees took the dive and made a killing as well.

Priceline and BiddingforTravel.com

This combination of websites in addition to Tripadvisor.com will save you over 50% on most of your hotel bookings from now on.

Priceline.com offers traditional booking services for airfare, hotel, car rental and vacation packages. Their "Name Your Own Price" feature is our key to saving money on every *hotel room* you book.

"Name Your Own Price" is an opaque booking site meaning you will not know for sure which hotel you will end up at. Don't let that scare you. Combined with BiddingForTravel.com and Tripadvisor.com, we can take the guesswork out of your bid, and get you a quality room in the location you want.

Here are steps that will give you an idea of what prices the hotels are accepting, at the quality level you demand, in the location you desire. This is a fantastic saving strategy:

Go to BiddingForTravel.com. Navigate to the hotel section and choose your destination city. Click on the Hotel list (at the top) for the city you are booking in. Write down each location name along with the highest star level available i.e. Airport 4 Star, Medford 3 Star etc. Remember, Resort is the highest category.

By accessing Tripadvisor.com you can read the reviews of hotels in the areas that are of interest to you.

Choose the lowest star level from Biddingfortravel you will accept in your desired location. If there is a bad hotel in the 3 star hotels listed, then you will want your minimum bidding category to be 3.5 stars. *You* control the quality of the room you will receive.

Once you have noted the lowest *acceptable hotel level* you will accept in your desired location, write down the names of all the other locations that have a *lower* star level listed as their highest level. If you choose a 3.5 star in your desired location, then only write down the names of the locations that have a highest star level of 3.0 or less. These extra locations will become your free rebids if your first offer is not accepted. Let's do a dry run.

Suppose your desired location within Anytown, USA is the *airport* location and you find all the hotel choices in the 3.5 star category would be acceptable to you. (No bad reviews). Looking at the other locations within the offerings, you note that *downtown* offers 4 star hotels, *Southside* offers 3.5 star hotels, *Eastside* offers 3.0 as the highest star level and Westside only has 2.5 as the highest level in the region. The only regions acceptable for a potential rebid would be *Eastside* and *Westside*. If you rebid *Southside* (they have a 3.5 start hotel), you could end up in Southside which is not acceptable to you.

Armed with your 2 free rebid zones go back to the Biddingfortravel page which listed acceptable bids for hotels in both the location and star category you are looking for. If you found an accepted bid in the airport zone for a 3.5 Star hotel at $48, you now have an idea of what prices are being accepted. There may be more than one accepted bid to review. There may be none, but you will get an idea of what the marketplace is accepting in the location you want and at the quality level you demand. Note that weekend stays typically accept lower bids than midweek, except in Las Vegas where the reverse is true.

You are now properly armed to try your first bid on Priceline.com. I have never been negatively surprised with the results from Priceline. *I do my homework first.* Remember when you bid, if accepted, your credit card will be charged immediately with no changes allowed. You are purchasing a hotel room right now. But you have the location and quality hotel you want and have reviewed other people's opinions of the properties. Do your homework *first.*

On Priceline.com navigate to the hotel section and then the Name your Own Price section. Type in the dates you want, the location you want and the star level you will accept. Now put in your bid price. Start low and as far in advance of your reservation as is practical. You are choosing only your desired location and a star level you will accept. Why not try a 4 Star in our example from above with a $45 starting bid.

You'll be asked to enter your credit card information and submit your bid. Remember, if accepted you have a non-refundable hotel reservation.

Let's assume you bid for a 4 Star in your desired location and the bid was refused. You can now bid 3.5 Stars (your lowest acceptable level) as a rebid. Up your bid a few bucks if you'd like. You do not have to. It is always your choice, but with each rebid you must change something about your request: different dates, add a location, or a different star level. (Changing *only the price* is not an acceptable change for a rebid.)

Again your bid of $48 was rejected and now it is time for another rebid. Add a zone that does not have a hotel at 3.5 Stars or higher (Eastside or Westside from our example) and up your bid to $52. If accepted you will end up in your original location (the only zone you are bidding on with a 3.5 Star hotel). If it doesn't work again, you still have one more free rebid, either Eastside or Westside, whichever one you did not use in your previous bid.

When you have used all your free rebids you are out of business for 24 hours before you can bid again. After 24 hours start the process over again until you score a winning bid. Typically a winning bid is about 50% of the normal hotel rate in the location you are looking for and at the quality level you demand.

Priceline does add taxes and fees to your bid, but you will see the total rate to be charged to your card before you actually hit "Buy my Hotel."

I have saved literally thousands of dollars using the Priceline, BiddingforTravel and Tripadvisor combination. It won't work in rural locations but it sure comes in handy when travelling to a major city.

Priceline's "Name Your Own Price" option is also a valuable tool for longer-term car rentals (five days plus). Use the same system as for hotels? The fee charged by Priceline eats up the savings on shorter car rentals, but it is well worth a try. You'll be amazed how cheaply you can rent a car.

Krakow, Poland

Best Rate Guarantees

This opportunity works for both hotel stays and airline tickets. The purpose of the vendor offering a guarantee is to entice you to book your room or flight directly with the vendor site you are viewing at that given moment. This guarantee states that if you find a better rate anywhere else online, your rate will be reduced to the competing rate and you'll be given a $ off discount voucher or coupon for a future stay or flight. Let's face it, there are so many booking sites that they need to entice you to use their service.

Look at hotel rooms for example. I know of at least 30 different sites where you can book a hotel room, in addition to the actual website of the hotel in question.

Historically the finest Best Rate Guarantee was offered by the Wyndham hotel program. Wyndham offered a free first night's stay if you found a better rate anywhere else on the Internet. Enterprising free hotel junkies would find acceptable lower rates, submit their guarantee requests and get their first night free. What Wyndham did not count on was that the guarantee junkies would only book one night at the hotel and then move on to another hotel, repeating the free night scenario.

I'm guilty as charged. One year when traveling from Traverse City, Michigan to Hilton Head Island, South Carolina for the winter, we took our time, as my bride had just undergone shoulder surgery and couldn't sit for long hours in the car. We took five nights to make the trip and I found a free Best Rate guarantee each and every night of the trip. Many reported staying numerous nights in the same city, and just hotel hopping from one free night to another.

Wyndham killed the bonanza and went to a more traditional award for finding a cheaper rate which consisted of matching the lower rate and providing a discount on a future stay. That reward and guarantee is now the norm with hotel Best Rate guarantees. A typical award would match the rate and provide a $50 off voucher for your next night if booked with the same site.

One of the shortcuts I've used to find viable Best Rate hotel guarantees is to use the multiple search sites to check more than one provider at a time. Here is an example: I want a room in Boston for a given night. I begin my search at Kayak.com or Hotelscombined.com because these give you the best available rates from up to 30 *different websites* with one search. If I find an acceptable hotel listed at $89 on Travelocity and $87 on Expedia.com, I have found a potential best rate guarantee to be filed with Travelocity. Travelocity's guarantee is to match the lower websites rate and give you a $50 voucher good for a future booking on Travelocity. My cost for this room night will be $87, the matched rate, but I'll have a $50 voucher for my next stay. In the future, I can apply my $50 voucher to a future reservation and even file another Best Rate guarantee claim if I can find one. The best source of online information for hotel best rate guarantees is called the Best Rate Guarantee Blog. Join their Google groups for daily updates of bargains they have found.

The airlines have been equally active with Best Rate guarantees. At the time of this printing both United Airlines and Continental (soon to be merged) offer a $100 guarantee if you find a lower airfare for the same flights on the same days within the same fare classes from another website (other than their own). The policy makes sense from an airline's standpoint. Airlines don't want to pay another online booking service a booking fee. Every airline wants to increase their percentage of captured reservations. It is economically in their best interest.

The great thing about these airline guarantees has been that they work for *one ways*. If you book two *one ways* instead of a round trip, you could acquire $200 in guarantees. Rules change constantly and you'll need to check the terms and conditions of the website Best Rate guarantee program.

There were numerous occasions when I have purchased tickets from the east coast to San Francisco as two *one way* tickets for around $100 each way. And with my accepted guarantees, have actually flown for free when figuring in my future vouchers. The best runs were flying free and then getting bumped off a flight and actually earning $200-$400. More about getting bumped in a later chapter.

The keys to earning the Best Rate guarantees are in *finding exactly the same terms and conditions between the websites.* The airlines, hotels and other booking sites offering Best Rate guarantees are *not* thrilled about issuing coupons and vouchers so they have some very strict guidelines. The terms, conditions and amenities of the hotel room must be an exact match. There is also a time component which requires you to file your claim typically within 24 hours of making your reservation. Some companies make you file your claim online. Others accept the claims by phone. I like the phone system better as you can find out if you have an accepted claim by the end of your phone call. The online claim can take several days to secure a response, and the company you are filing the claim with can always say they could not find the competing websites better price. I want to know *immediately* if I have been successful.

The Best Rate reservation does not have to be prepaid to qualify. You need to be careful to make that distinction when reserving your room with the company you plan to file a claim against. If you prepaid for the room, you own that reservation regardless if your claim is approved or not.

The better system, and the one I like to use, is to first find the better rate that I will be using before I even make my reservation. I use this information when making the reservation with the company offering the Best Rate guarantee. The reservation will not be prepaid and I'll try to do business with companies that will answer my claim request on the phone immediately when I file the claim.

Budapest, Hungary

Voluntary Denied Boarding or the "Bump"

Nothing gets my heart racing (well almost nothing) like a free trip to somewhere. This is a fun topic for me, because I enjoy this benefit of frugal travel soooo much. **The Bump.**

Airlines sell more seats for each flight than the plane will accommodate. Why? Because some people won't show up for their flights. Others actually fly on expensive refundable tickets. (Huh) Some invoke the "spare tire" rule effectively allowing them to fly a later time on the same day. And sometimes with irregular operations, maybe weather, the airlines just sell more seats than they can accommodate. There are numerous situations that justify an airline "overselling" a flight. From the airlines' perspective, if a seat goes out empty, it means lost revenue they can never recover.

Airlines are mandated by law to compensate those passengers that are denied boarding because a flight is oversold. If 102 people show up for a flight capable of carrying 100, two people will not get on that plane. They will either volunteer to give up their seat, or the airline will chose who stays behind.

A Frugal Traveler with *"flexible travel plans"* will volunteer to take a later flight in return for just compensation. A smart Frugal Traveler will understand the system in order to increase their chances of *The Bump*.

The keys to success are:

Have flexible travel plans. Don't be in such a rush. Make the travel day, a travel day.

Take carryon luggage only. The airlines are more apt to pick you, if they don't have to unload your bag.

Pick flights that are full or close to full. For example Friday, Sunday and Monday generally provide the best opportunities to Bump. Also, the days around holidays or major events will be terrific opportunities to *Bump*. There will be hundreds of denied boardings around the Super Bowl, the Comdex convention in Las Vegas, and the Final Four Basketball weekend.

If possible, schedule travel well in advance to take advantage of schedule changes. Example: your flights for 6 months from now have a schedule change, and the airline calls you to "reconfirm" you. You can now pick the fullest flights for that route, thereby increasing your odds of *The Bump*.

If you are travelling with others in your party, decide beforehand if you are willing to split up and have one or two stay behind, to board later, and the others go on, depending on whatever the airline needs in terms of volunteers.

And most importantly, be the first one to volunteer. I take two steps to make sure this happens.

When I leave my departure city I check

with the ticket agent to see if I can volunteer for all segments of my itinerary. I have a real leg up on the competition if I can volunteer at 7AM for flight later in my itinerary that departs at say 4PM. Most of the other travelers have not even checked in at this point.

I'm first at the actual departure gate. Most gate agents show up 1 hour before scheduled flight time. I get to the gate at 1 hour and 15 minutes before departure and read the local paper or use my computer right at the podium until they show up.

I stand at the counter and patiently wait for the gate agent to arrive and do his/her initial computer start up. When he/she asks "may I help you" I offer to volunteer by asking if they will be needing volunteers or if the flight is oversold. If "yes" or "maybe" is the answer, tell them your name and ask to be put on the volunteer list. This is not a commitment to volunteer, but puts you in first place when it is time to negotiate the compensation. The agent may ask if I have checked baggage, the city of my final destination and I gladly provide the information. Then I leave them alone. I check back with the gate agent about 15 minutes before departure to see if he/she wants me to wait to board the plane. If the answer is "wait" I ask what the compensation will be if I'm needed. The last few minutes before departure are fun for me, as I wait to see if I'm going. I have a list of alternate flights that I can use, and have a general idea of the compensation the airline will be offering for denied boarding.

Before I accept the denied boarding compensation, and for sure before the flight actually leaves, I find out which alternate flights I will be given a confirmed reservation on, and the actual compensation being offered.

In our example, the agent tells me to wait and I actually do get *The Bump*. I'm going to be compensated for my flexible travel plans. Most airlines will try to offer you a free domestic ticket and a seat on the next flight. I usually resist this compensation as the free ticket is capacity controlled, just like award tickets, and pays no frequent flyer miles when you use it. I prefer $$ off vouchers from the airline. A typical offer would be a $400 voucher, good for future travel anywhere on that airline. If the delay until the next flight is a long one, the compensation offered will be increased. If they are way oversold, it will take more $$$ to get people off the flight and they will up the offer of compensation. You should always demand the same compensation as the highest paid volunteer. You'll get it. Also, the longer the delay the higher the compensation the airlines are required to provide you. Recent legislative changes being considered include the possibility of receiving $650 for delays of fewer than 4 hours and $1300 for longer delays. I can buy quite a few airline tickets with $1300 in bump vouchers.

Ask for the "goodies." If you are being delayed a long time, ask for an amenity pack which will include a phone card, food vouchers and maybe a few frequent flyer miles. If you are forced to stay overnight, the airlines will pay for your accommodations and meals. If they forget to offer, remind them. And my favorite goodie is to ask to be moved up to first class on the later flight. If they have the seats, you'll get one and if the agent is in haste when reticketing you, sometimes they code that seat as a purchased first class ticket and you get the class of service bonus miles as well. *You are in the driver's seat.* The airlines need your seat and you can bargain, but be *courteous and appreciative* of the agent's efforts on your behalf.

So how lucrative can this be? One afternoon I arrived in Atlanta at 4 PM for my connecting flight to Savannah, Georgia. I was bumped off the 5PM flight, 7PM flight, 9PM flight and the 11PM flight before it even arrived in Atlanta. I was also bumped off the first flight in the morning and finally (darn it) boarded the second flight the next morning. My compensation for an 18-hour delay was eight domestic tickets, good for anywhere in the USA. I was given food money and a hotel. The value of those eight tickets if used properly is $2500++.

On a recent trip to Anchorage Alaska I had paid $400 for the round trip ticket and received four $400 vouchers for successive *bumps* along the way. I actually flew to Alaska and made $1200 for my effort.

On a return flight from Hawaii we arrived in Chicago to find an oversold flight to Savannah.

The next flight offering confirmable seats was more than 4 hours later, hence we were entitled to increased compensation and the gate agent knew his stuff. We respectfully stayed out of his way and let him board his flight before dealing with us. He gave us a total of $1200 in vouchers ($600 each). We then asked if he could put Katy on a flight to Columbia South Carolina to be with her daughter and he put her on one leaving in less than an hour later. He then proceeded to put me on the standby list for the next flight to Savannah which left in less than two hours and I made that flight as well. I was compensated $1200, saved myself driving 3 and a half hours to get Katy to Columbia and only waited 2 extra hours to fly home.

Agents will work with you if you are courteous, patient and knowledgeable.

International denied boardings can really pay off. It is not unusual to be offered $750 to $1000 in vouchers for denied boarding. Add that up for a family of four bumped off flights two or three times in succession and you will be flying for free for a year.

A few final tips on "Bumps" — Always ask. Never miss the opportunity to get paid to wait. I have received bumps flying mid-day, mid-week from Chicago to Jacksonville, of all places. You have no control over weather, excess baggage, and other cancelled flights that may oversell your flight. You will not be compensated unless you ask. Be proactive in volunteering.

And lastly, in hot or humid weather, the airplanes ability to "lift" is affected and not as much weight can be carried. Flights are booked to capacity, but "weight restrictions" require the off loading of passengers and freight. Darn it, we get paid again.

BumpFests happen all the time. If you have flexible plans and can take multiple consecutive bumps, you may earn enough in vouchers or free tickets to fly for free the rest of the year.

Good Luck

Acropolis - Greece

"Eggo Waffles and Magazines for Everyone"

In 2004, Kellogg the maker of Eggo Waffles, offered boxes of 10 frozen waffles with a 100 American Airlines coupon on the side of the box. The promotion required a minimum of five boxes for redemption of 500 miles. That minimum was not a problem.

Frequent flyer miles in 2004 were worth close to 2 cents per mile so 10 waffles offered at the large discount stores like Target, Sam's Club etc at under $2 were a bargain. Kellogg had actually been running the promo for several years but it wasn't until a product hit this price point that things really heated up.

The lowest price I found was $1.89, and I had some 50 cent off coupons that brought my price down to $1.39 per hundred AA miles with 10 waffles thrown in basically for free. I bought all I could for several months, cut off the coupon and delivered the boxes of waffles to the local homeless shelter where they were a welcome sight. Everyone was a big winner with this promo.

The magazine promotion came from ValueMags, an online retailer of magazine subscriptions. They attempted to back out on paying the miles but I was successful at receiving 112.5 miles for every dollar I spent on magazine subscriptions. You wanted a magazine, you received 3 years worth. Christmas, birthdays, for any reason at all, that year you got magazines. The best use was when I ordered them for the Veterans Clinics around Michigan for reading in their waiting rooms. My son's school library received any magazine subscription they wanted for the library as well. I got a tax deduction to boot.

Online magazine subscription sites still offer miles in large quantities. I see offers for 50 miles per dollar quite often. If you want the magazines anyway, search the airline shopping malls for these offers.

Customer Service Vouchers and Miles

We all know that the quality of commercial airline service has declined significantly in the last several decades. Although the airlines need to cut costs to make a profit, they still are responsible for providing the basic product of efficient, reliable transportation. At times it just does not happen that way. When service falls short, it is our responsibility and opportunity to request compensation for the airlines' shortcomings.

If a stereo system doesn't work, the lavatory is out of service, your seat breaks, they lose your luggage, the movie doesn't work, the air vents hum too loudly, you have the right to register a complaint and expect compensation.

Most of the above examples have happened in my years in the air and I've found the airlines quite reasonable in compensating me for their shortcomings. In fact, at times, they have compensated me with more than the cost of my ticket.

Every airline website includes a Customer Relations department for registering complaints and also to provide a compliment for a job well done. I have used airline websites and at other times mailed a letter to Customer Relations. I have experienced success with both methods.

The information required includes: the actual ticket number, confirmation number, departure city, arrival city, date of flight and the flight number. You'll find this on your boarding pass. I keep my boarding passes until my frequent flyer miles post, so I always have the information available if I need to submit a complaint.

Make your request factual indicating how the problem negatively affected your travel experience, but always be polite and professional in your approach. My letters look something like this:

"On flight 123, May 8th from Chicago to Denver I had the unfortunate experience of flying without an operating audio system. The flight time seemed to drag on forever without the entertainment system"

I know that XYZ Airlines prides itself on providing a quality product and felt it necessary to let you know of my disappointment. As a Premier member of your airline frequent flyer program, I have had many successful trips, but think in light of the circumstances, some sort of compensation is due for the broken audio system.

I will leave the amount of compensation to your best judgment and assure you that based on a satisfactory resolution to this matter; I will continue to fly XYZ Airlines.

I look forward to your response and a continued positive customer relationship.

Respectfully"

Some people demand a specific compensation. I think it best to leave it to the airline if you are a frequent flyer with them. Compensation can come in the form of frequent flyer miles deposited to your account, a discount voucher for future travel or a dollar amount discount based on the amount of your next ticket purchase ($50 off a ticket of $200 or more, $75 off a ticket of $300 or more).

My past compensations have included 10,000 miles for a non-working lavatory, $50 for a broken seat, $200 for a poor television system and $250 for a reroute to a different airport than anticipated (plus all costs). The $250 for the reroute to another airport happened while trying to fly to Boise, Idaho. The flight left late due to crew delays and when we made an approach to Boise, the weather minimums forced us to land in Idaho Falls. Weather issues are not usually reason for compensation, but I think the airline knew that we would never land in Boise. When I checked my email upon my hotel arrival, I found a $250 electronic certificate in my email.

The plan was to stay in an Idaho Falls hotel for that evening and returned to the airport for the continuing short flight to Boise in the morning. Weather again delayed our departure. The purpose of my trip was solely to earn miles and visiting a state I'd never been to. At this point I requested to be rerouted back home and my wish was granted. To top off the $250 voucher, I was bumped off the flight from Denver to

Chicago, spent an extra two hours in the airport and earned an additional $400 voucher. My original ticket cost $34 using a previously earned $200 voucher. I had earned the miles, been bumped up to first class on the return and made $650 in vouchers. Some trips go very well, even if you don't get where you want to go.

This technique for earning additional miles or vouchers should not be used with every flight. But every time you have an issue you should report it to the airline. If you are polite and not overly demanding, you'll be amazed at how hard they will work to retain your business.

And again, a word of thanks for a job well done should be sent when things go well or you encounter an exceptionally good employee. They work hard for us.

Frequent Flyer Miles:
Definitions and Distinctions

The backbone of frugal travel is the judicious collection of miles and points at a wholesale value or less, and the ultimate use of your hoard of miles and points at a much higher value. Let's start with some distinctions.

Frequent flyer miles are awarded by the airline programs such as American Aadvantage, Continental OnePass, Delta Skymiles, United Mileage Plus, US Airways Dividend Miles and others based upon the completion of activities associated with their awards program. These activities could include flying on the airline or one of its partner airlines, using a debit or credit card from a partner bank, or shopping with merchants within the airlines online shopping mall. In addition, partners could be rental car companies, stock and bond brokerage firms, restaurants and hotels booked through the affiliated RewardsNetwork program, Internet service providers and cell phone companies or even dry cleaning firms. If you use an affiliated credit card to make any type of purchase, frequent flyer miles can be earned for almost every transaction you are involved in. Miles and points are all around us. It is literally raining miles and points if you look for them.

Some airlines, such as Southwest Airlines and Airtran, use a "credits" system whereby the above mentioned activities earn "credits" instead of miles.

Hotel programs such as Hyatt, Hilton, Marriott, Wyndham, Sheraton and others issue hotel points for activities similar to those of the airlines. The difference is that you earn hotel **points** for staying in the hotels and acting within their awards program and you earn **miles** for flying on the airlines and participating with their partners.

Lastly, we have the awards programs of various banks and credit cards that are not associated directly with an airline or hotel program. Examples would be Citi Thank You Points, Chase Ultimate Rewards, Bank of America Worldpoints, US Bank Flexperks, and American Express Membership Rewards points. Again, these are referred to as rewards points but are distinct and different from hotel points.

The reason for these programs existence is twofold. The first is to induce your loyalty. The philosophy of marketing is that if you fly on American Airlines and earn frequent flyer miles for that activity, you will continue to use that airline or their affiliated marketing partners until you have earned enough miles to claim an award.

The second reason for the programs is that they are extremely profitable programs for the airlines in particular. Airlines sell their frequent flyer miles to their affiliates who in turn use them in turn to create loyalty within their own business. For example, Citibank buys literally millions of dollars of American Airlines Aadvantage miles each year with the hopes you will use their credit card to make your purchases. You earn miles with your credit card purchases and for your loyalty; they can charge you interest and fees if you don't pay your credit card bill off in full each month. It is a Win-Win for both parties.

Our part in this equation as consumers is to earn miles, points and rewards for our normal day to day activities at no extra cost. And at times, reap an award bonanza for activities within these airline, hotel or bank rewards programs. Here is an example of what I mean by an award bonanza. This was a hugely successful one for me.

One of the hotel award programs is called Goldpoints Plus and is the rewards program for the Radisson, Country Inns & Suites, Park Inn and Park Plaza hotel chains. They have an online shopping mall. If you make purchases through their online mall with their affiliated retail partners you earned Goldpoints. One of their partners was Shutterfly, an online photo development firm. As a promotion to introduce their new relationship with the Goldpoints Rewards program, Shutterfly offered 1500 Goldpoints for any online purchase. Keep in mind that 15,000 Goldpoints was necessary for redemption of a lower end hotel night during this promotion. If I made 10 purchases from Shutterfly I would earn enough points for a hotel night.

The least expensive purchase on Shutterfly was for the printing of one 4" x 6" picture. The cost was 39 cents. To have the photo shipped was another $1.50 for a total purchase price of $1.89. If I did this 10 times I would have enough points for a free hotel stay. Well not free, but $18.90 per night. I like hotel stays that cost $18.90 per night.

I made over 700 purchases of $1.89 for a total cost of $1323.00 and received over 1 million Goldpoints for my effort. The orders were easy to make while watching the evening news, or sitting in the coffee shop. It took about 4 clicks for each order and I had fun sending multiple copies of the same photo to friends. They thought I was crazy. Crazy like a fox as it turned out.

I redeemed many of the points at lower end hotels for a net cost of $18.90 per room. My best use of the points was at the high end Radisson in Edinburgh, Scotland. The room was available for 250 euros (about $400 at the time), or 60,000 Goldpoints. I chose the Goldpoints award, which based on my acquisition costs of $18.90 x 4, was less than $80. The best part of that redemption was they forgot to take the 60,000 points from my account. My stay was free as the 60,000 points was never deducted.

I never violated the terms of the promotion. I just used it to my advantage. There are more "stories" of success throughout the book.

The Value of Miles and Points

I'd love to give you a fixed value for each type of airline mile, hotel point or bank rewards point. But they vary in value to each individual using them, based on their travel style and the maximum an individual would pay for a given product. Here is an example of what I mean:

To a business man that needs to fly New York to London in two weeks time, and wants to fly in Business Class, he may be willing to pay $5000 for a round trip ticket. If the business traveler could get that ticket for 100,000 frequent flyer miles, he would be receiving a value of 5 cents per frequent flyer mile spent. He may or may not redeem his miles for the ticket.

To a leisure traveler who is willing to fly coach he would probably have to pay $1000 for that ticket in summer season and could redeem 50,000 miles for the ticket. His return is only 2 cents per frequent flyer mile spent but he still may redeem his miles if the return is satisfactory for his or her needs and travel style.

For years, people used the 2 cents per point guideline as a value of a frequent flyer mile. I personally think that is high with the recent devaluation of the airline award charts but still not too bad of a guideline for redeeming your miles. If I can acquire airline miles at less than 1 cent each (free is my favorite) and redeem them for more than 2 cents each, I am a big winner.

Different airline miles actually have different values to collectors based on several factors. Ease of award availability is a big factor in the value of miles. Delta Airlines has recently had the value of their miles decrease among serious collectors because using the awards has become so difficult. Delta has further devalued their miles by instituting a three-tier award chart requiring more miles to be redeemed than for equivalent trips on competitor airlines.

Other factors that influence the value of frequent flyer miles are the rules, terms and conditions of use of the airline program award. An award ticket that allows a free stopover in an intermediate city has more value than an award ticket that does not. The ability to do an open jaw and one way awards within an airline award program also positively affects the value of the miles.

Hotel points vary greatly in value because of the variation in the amount of points necessary to receive a free hotel night. A low level room with Starwood can be had for 3000 points while it takes 12,000 to 15,000 points for a low level Hilton room stay. In fairness to those programs that charge more points for a nights stay, their credit cards earn multiple points per dollar spent in some categories and the actual paid stay earns more points as well. A great source of information on the relative value of hotel points is the Loyalty Traveler blog by Ric Garrido. He seems to have the best handle on the true value and real bargains in the hotel reward industry.

Here is my simple example of how I decide to pay cash or use points for a hotel night.

I use as my "day to day" credit card the Starwood Preferred Guest card by American Express. My cost of acquiring SPG points is $0.00 as I do not pay for the points I accumulate, I simply gather them by using the credit card. When I have accumulated 3000 points by spending $3000 of normal and typical purchases (1 point earned per dollar spent on the card) I can redeem those points for a night at a lower end Starwood property like a Four Points by Sheraton. The typical cost of the room is about $120 per night. I am receiving a value of 4 cents per point when I make that redemption. I like that redemption return on investment and use it as a guideline for myself. If the room is less than $120 I may pay cash. If more, than redeeming my points is the right way for me to go.

In this example, I value my SPG points at 4 cents each.

Bank Rewards Points

These points are much easier to value as the redemption value is typically set by the bank at 1 cent per point. The banks have merchandise, gift cards and air travel available for redemption and they all seem to run around one cent per point each. If your bank credit card gives you one point per dollar spent, I think you can see why I use the SPG card which has a value per point of around 2.5 to 3 cents each.

In defense of the bank rewards points they sometimes offer category bonuses which equate to more points earned per dollar spent in certain categories. It is not uncommon for a bank reward credit card to award 3-5 points per dollar spent for gas, grocery or drugstore purchases. There are other bonus categories as well, as determined by the rewards program of the bank.

Many bank rewards points can be converted to airline miles at a 1 to 1 ratio. In some circumstances this can be a very good use of your bank rewards points.

Elite Qualifying Miles and Elite Status

Let's first address the difference between a Revenue Mile (RDM) and an (EQM) Elite Qualifying mile. You earn revenue miles for everything you do within the awards program. Revenue miles are earned when rent a car. Using your credit card will earn you revenue miles. When you fly, you earn Revenue Miles (RDM) and Elite Qualifying Miles (EQM).

Elite Qualifying Miles are earned by flying Butt-in-Seat. It takes Elite Qualifying Miles (EQM) to increase your status level within an airline program.

Airlines have designed this system to reward their best customers. Each airline has established several levels of elite status based upon actual flight activity. The miles that are awarded for flying are called Elite Qualifying Miles or Medallion Miles by Delta Airlines. I like to refer to them as *Butt-in-Seat* miles as that is typically the only way to earn them.

Elite status levels are often designated by a metal name: Silver, Gold, Platinum, etc. Each airline has its own unique set of qualifying guidelines and elite status names. For *United Airlines* the levels are Base Member, Premier Associate (you purchase this one), Premier, Premier Executive, 1K and Global Services. For *Delta Airlines* levels include Silver, Gold, Platinum and Diamond and *American Airlines* has Gold, Platinum and Executive Platinum.

The lowest status level attained by flying typically happens at 25,000 *elite qualifying miles* or *Butt-in-Seat* miles. Once a level is reached within a calendar year your status is bumped up from general member to the first level, and you are now granted some goodies when you fly. The most common goodie is that flying actually earns you more miles. In most programs as a base member, if you fly 600 miles, you earn 600 miles (RDM and 600 EQM) in your frequent flyer account. At the lowest Elite level you'll typically earn an elite bonus of 25% more miles or in our example 600 miles + 125 miles (RDM). The elite qualifying miles earned still remain 600 miles but you now have 725 miles (RDM) available for award redemptions in the future.

The second tier is usually reached when you hit 50,000 Elite Qualifying miles. Your bonus in revenue miles then increases to 100% so our sample flight would still earn 600 EQM as well as 1200 revenue miles (RDM).

The higher your status level the better the bennies. In addition to extra revenue miles you will receive confirmed upgrades to the next class of service on domestic flights, the ability to reserve exit row seats or premium coach seats at the time of ticketing, unlimited upgrades based on availability, international upgrades and lounge access on international itineraries. One of the best benefits is the additional assistance in the event of irregular operations. When things go wrong, and with airlines they do, they take care of their best customers first. I have even received higher financial compensation for unsatisfactory operations as a high-tier elite. The absolute top tiers in the various programs are usually by invitation only and reserved for the very best spenders on the airline. The perks for this status level are reminiscent of the good old days in airline travel. You are first in line for all the airline's services.

Unlike the revenue miles earned for all activities within a frequent flyer program, elite qualifying miles expire every year. If you earn Gold Status with an airline in 2011 it will be active for the remainder of 2011 and all of 2012. The expiration of the benefits will be typically in February 2013. But your earning period for Elite Qualifying miles is the calendar year. January 1 —December 31.

Many of us find ourselves just short of the next elite level as we near the end of the calendar year and will actually fly a **mileage run** just to gather the EQM required to move us to that next level. A **mileage run** is flown with no purpose other than to obtain Elite Qualifying miles. At times this will make great financial sense. As a footnote, there are instances where a credit card company will grant you elite qualifying miles when you reach a certain spending amount within a calendar year, or after paying a large annual fee. These offers tend to be expensive but can be helpful in reaching that next elite status level.

Hotel rewards programs also recognize and grant status for the number of nights or stays within a calendar year. The more stays or nights, the higher your status level and the bigger the benefits you are awarded. The benefits include room upgrades, extra hotel points (similar to what we saw in the airlines' programs), late checkout, free breakfasts and free Internet usage. One of my favorite benefits of hotel status is the use of a dedicated lounge where there are quite often complimentary cocktails and snacks. Some of the snack spreads are as nice as many dinner buffets.

Transferring Hotel Points and Airline Miles

Transferring hotel points to airline miles is an area with significant variations in transfer rates. My favorite hotel points (SPG) can be transferred to American Airlines at a ratio of 1:1, plus a 5000-mile bonus when transferring 20,000 points at a time. This same transfer to United Airlines is 2:1. Neither of these are particularly attractive options, but the transfer to United miles is extremely disastrous. Other hotel programs transfer their points to airlines at 5:1. Again a real loser for those collecting either miles or points.

The reverse of this, the transfer of airline miles to hotel points, is again one that offers a wide range of values. For example, you can transfer one American Airlines mile into the Hilton Honors program and receive 2 Hilton Honors points 1:2. It may seem like a reasonable transfer to some, but if you can use your American miles for a premium class award ticket, you will find the value of your AA miles to be considerably higher.

Caution should be used when considering transfers between programs, and websites that specialize in transfers such as Points.com may show some even worse ratios. Be *careful* with your hard earned points and miles. You are the ultimate decision maker on how and where to use them. Be aware that transfers are almost always non-cancellable.

My favorite "Points Transfer" story includes a cast of characters starring Amex Rewards points, SPG points and Continental Airlines miles. The first step was to transfer 25,000 of any of the above points to the Amtrak Guest Rewards program without limit.

The second step involved transferring Amtrak Guest Rewards points to Choice Hotel points. The transfer ratio was extremely favorable and again unlimited. If my memory serves me correctly the transfer was 1 Amtrak point to 5 Choice points. The third transfer was Choice hotel points to Southwest Airlines Rapid Rewards airline tickets. The final outcome? 25,000 of the original points transformed into 3.67 round trip Rapid Rewards tickets.

I split my transfer winnings between Rapid Rewards tickets for some family members and hotel points for us. In the end we ended up with 7 or 8 free (or almost free) airline tickets and over 1 million Choice Hotel reward points amongst my immediate family members.

This story has a moral to it:
"If a deal is so good you can't resist, load up for everybody in the family."

The website Webflyer.com has a section named "Mileage Converter" that reflects the current transfer options between all the active hotel and airline programs as well as the American Express Membership Rewards program. I find it to be a useful tool when wondering how and where I can move my orphan miles and points.

Hunta Kora Bone Church
Czech Republic

Rewards Network Bonus Miles

Every airline frequent flyer program and some of the hotel chains have a partnership with the RewardsNetwork which lists registered restaurants and hotels around the USA. These restaurants and hotels pay frequent flyer miles above and beyond the 1 mile per dollar spent on your rewards credit card.

Once you register your credit card with the network simply use that card when dining at an enrolled restaurant or staying at an enrolled hotel. (See the search function on the RewardsNetwork site for restaurants in your area). There are restaurants in almost every location.

PLEASE NOTE: Some restaurants have limited days of participation (no Friday or Saturday bonus).

Based on your level of participation, you will receive 1, 3 or 5 miles per dollar spent in addition to the mile for the credit card charge. In addition, there are frequently bonuses above the base earnings, especially for new members.

Examples are spending a minimum within a certain time frame or just "double ups" for activity in the program.

If you are not a member of a particular frequent flyer program, sign up for the airline program first, then sign up with the RewardsNetwork affiliate for that airline.

When you sign up, be sure to fill out an online profile and register at least one unique credit card to that program. It makes sense to register your Citi American Airlines Credit Card with the AA arm of the Rewardsnetwork, but you don't have to. Likewise it makes sense to sign up your United Mileage Plus card with the United Airlines division of RewardsNetwork. You can register any card you want, but let's use the K.I.S.S. system and Keep it Simple Sweetheart.

REMEMBER: Each credit card can only be registered with one Rewardsnetwork program.
For a casual user (less than 12 dines per year) you will receive an extra 3 miles per dollar plus the original one mile for using your airline's affiliated credit card. To reach the 3 mile per dollar level you must create an online profile with RewardsNetwork. If you don't, you will earn only one extra mile per dollar spent.

For those that dine out frequently, the bonus is an extra 5 miles per dollar. Remember, we are talking about free miles here.

When the bonuses are right I have used this program aggressively, meaning weekly. Occasionally I'll find an offer of 20 miles per dollar spent. When that happens I'll buy a $600 gift card from the restaurant I frequent anyway. I can pick up an extra 12,000 miles for a restaurant gift card, that I know I will make use of.

With the RewardsNetwork you also have the option of earning "cash back", but what fun would that be?

Now, when you go out to lunch with a friend or business associates, have them pay you in cash for their share, and put the entire bill on your airline credit card. You win, they don't care, and you're closer to flying for free.

PS: Rewardsnetwork also pays 5 miles per dollar on your hotel bookings with their participating hotels. I have never tried it, as I can always do better with the Priceline, Biddingfortravel and Tripadvisor trick I described earlier in the book.

Venice, Italy

Credit Cards

This technique is NOT for everyone. At the outset of this section it must be made clear that:

"Your credit is one of your most important assets"

Credit should not to be abused in order to collect frequent flyer miles and points. The ability to buy a home, automobile or pay for a college education will provide substantially more benefit in your lifetime than a few miles. If there has to be a reason to maintain your good credit, choose the home, car or education. But, I hope to show you how it is possible to have all of the above.

It is possible to use your good credit to obtain free travel. Lots of free travel. My good credit has been responsible for the largest percentage of my frequent flyer mile accrual. Credit card companies, in their attempt to lure you to use their product, offer huge sign up bonuses for applying, being approved and using their credit cards. A typical sign up bonus is equal to a free roundtrip domestic ticket, with no annual fee required the first year. I have applied for credit cards for years, fulfilled the requirements to achieve the sign up bonus and never used that card again. There are literally hundreds of rewards travel cards available. Some companies still let you have more than one of the same credit card and will give you the sign-up bonus each time you apply. These are disappearing rapidly though. It is becoming a "One time, One sign up bonus world". I have applied for and received over 90 credit cards to date. My scores are still in the "good credit" range. Now, back to our plan.

Every one of us is rated by all three of the credit reporting agencies based on our past credit history. We have a credit report on file that lists our past credit activity and a credit score assigned to us based on our past credit performance.

The three reporting agencies are Equifax, Transunion and Experian. Credit lenders hire one of these 3 agencies to send them a report on your past credit when you apply for a loan or credit card and also to send along their rating of your credit in the form of a credit score. The higher the score, the better your credit according to the agency.

It is important for you to review your credit report and credit score frequently. It has been reported that over 10% of all credit reports have errors on them that negatively affect your credit score. Make sure the information is correct on your report. I offer links on my blog for "free credit score trial offers" if you cancel within the 7 day trial offer period. Many of those offers will also include a copy of your credit report.

There are currently two scales of credit scores, FICO and VantageScore. The FICO scale runs from 300 to a high of 850. An acceptable score is above 660 and a good score is above 700. The VantageScore system runs from 501 to a high of 990. In years past, the FICO scale has been the most common although the newer VantageScore scale comes with an easy to understand letter grading system as well, and is gaining prominence in the lending community.

901 to 990 – A
801 to 900 – B
701 to 800 – C
601 to 700 – D
501 to 600 – F

For purposes of discussion let's stay with the old standby, the FICO system and the belief that a score of 700 and above is a good credit score.

What most people fail to realize is that if you have a credit score that is 720 or 780 or 850, your loan request will be approved all other factors being considered. It is not necessary to have a perfect score, just a good score. Making your payments on time, keeping your balances at less than 50% of available credit and not applying for too many loans or cards within a short time frame are the important factors that affect your ability to be approved. If you agree to make your payments on time and not use more than 50% of your credit lines at any one time, you can control your scores by controlling the number of credit inquiries received by each of the credit reporting agencies. Here is an example:

Your past credit history and current financial

situation have your credit scores on the FICO scale at 710 on Equifax, 740 on Transunion and 680 on Experian. Each agency uses their own formula and the scores will be different. Expect it and use it to your benefit. If 700-720 is a good score it appears you have a higher than needed score with Transunion. If you apply for a credit card from a lender that uses Transunion's information, expect your credit score to be reduced 2 to 5 points. Too many inquiries can be a reason for loan or card denial. To lenders, it means you are taking on too much new debt or may need more credit to support your lifestyle.

My example suggests that we want our scores to always be above 700-720 and the inquiry at Transunion will not affect your score with Equifax or Experian as long as you pay on time and keep your balances below the 50% of the credit limit level. The new card will eventually be seen by Equifax and Experian but if you use it properly it will not negatively affect your score.

After you receive your new credit card, your scores remain the same with Equifax and Experian and your score will fall to approximately 735 with Transunion.

Each credit inquiry is reflected in your credit score for 2 years and has a negative effect for that time period. If you use our example above and assume a 5 point hit to your credit score for every inquiry, you could apply for 8 credit cards in a two year time span with lenders that use

Transunion and your score would not fall below 700, our magic "good credit score" number.

Determining which credit reporting agency that will be checking your credit is not an exact science. The internet gives us a glimpse of which lenders use which agencies to secure their credit reports. I use a website called creditboards.com. After joining (free) and logging in I proceed to the *forum sections* then to the *credit pulls database* which lists lenders and the agencies they utilize in your state of residence. Try the exercise with me. Let's assume you live in New York State and want to apply for my favorite card the SPG card by American Express. I start by logging into creditboards.com, moving to the forums and the credit pulls database. I can now enter the information I know for sure (New York and American Express as the card issuer). The results, although not 100% conclusive, seem to indicate that in New York state most applications for an American Express card are checked by Experian.

With this information available to you, you can now plan your credit card applications based on lender and credit reporting agency.

The Citicard Bonanza

For many years Citibank has been aligned with the American Airlines Aadvantage program. They offered at least 5 different credit cards offering sign up bonuses of 25,000 to 30,000

American Airlines miles upon approval and fulfilling the minimum spend requirements. Citibank went for years allowing borrowers to apply for multiple cards, collect the bonus, cancel the card, reapply for the same card again and receive another sign up bonus. It was a real gravy train of miles and one that Katy and I took advantage of often. Our first of two Around the World itineraries were obtained from Citicard sign up bonuses. We needed 150,000 AA miles each to book an Around the World ticket that would allow us travel up to 25,000 flight miles in Business Class. That represented six (6) credit card sign up bonuses. A feat we were able to attain easily in one year.

In recent years Citibank has ceased the "free candy counter" but people still report isolated cases of multiple approvals. My last binge was five (5) credit card applications with Citi in one day in November 2009 that resulted in four (4) approvals and 100,000 American Airlines miles.

With the bonanza at Citi and other card issuers tightening up it is important to use the system I described before the Citi card story. Rotating your card applications between lenders that use different credit reporting agencies allows you to keep your scores above the *good range* while the inquiries melt away in two years time. If I could find enough good sign up bonuses on new cards, I could apply for about 4-6 cards every 90 days and never move my credit scores out of the "good range". One or two inquiries per agency every 90 days is eight (8) in two year's time or a maximum hit on my score of about 40 points. With my usual credit scores running in the 750-760 range I can follow this formula and still maintain a 700-720 score.

The things I consider when deciding which cards to apply for are the size of the sign up bonus and the probability I will use the award. A sign-up bonus worth one night's hotel stay does not excite me. I want a significant value for the 2-5 points my credit score will drop. Partial awards in obscure programs are also out. What good is a 10,000 mile sign up bonus in a program where it takes 25,000 miles for an award and I have little or no chance of achieving the minimum?

I also consider the cost of the card. Is the first year fee waived or am I required paying it? If I have the choice of spending $85 on a first year fee or applying for a card where the fee is waived, you know which way I am going to go.

And my last major consideration is the required "minimum spend" to achieve the award. I can easily spend $750 in day to day spending to qualify for an award. But when this requires thousands of dollars, I'm hesitant to do so. What I want is the sign up bonus award, without using this card for my everyday purchases. Most of the time I will never earn a second award with the same card.

Even with careful planning, making all payments on time, and keeping your utilization under 50%, credit card applications get denied. You have just reached a disagreement with the card issuer. Nobody is mad at you and the denial in itself does not hurt your credit score. You just need to restate your case to the credit card company with a "reconsideration letter".

When you receive a denial for a credit card application, you will be sent an email or snail mail letter giving the reasons for denial. The letter will also include a reference number for you to use when asking for reconsideration. I cannot remember ever having my reconsideration request denied. Here are two samples of letters I send:

Reconsideration Request

Case # 123456789

Your denial came as a surprise to me for the following reasons:

I am gainfully employed earning $xxx per year with no long term debt. (Or list the minimum debt you have)

I have had credit cards for xxx years and have **NEVER BEEN LATE** with a payment.

My current credit score is XXX as I checked it myself and that is in the GOOD range.

I am requesting reconsideration for your minimum line of credit to prove to you my credit worthiness. I look forward to receiving your card in the near future.

Respectfully,

Second Successful Sample

RE: Credit Card Reconsideration Request

To Whom It May Concern:

I was surprised to receive an online denial of my recent SPG Amex card application reference # 123456987654.
I am asking you to reconsider your decision based on the following facts:

My wife and I are both employed full time as professionals and have an annual income in excess of $_____.

Although our past credit is limited, you can see from our credit report, we have never missed a payment nor been late. I know, as I checked my credit score just before applying for your card to insure its accuracy. I note the current credit score is 745 which is better than over 55% of the public and is considered good credit by the credit reporting agency.

We are not heavy users of credit and never plan to be, but have heard from many sources that your card is the best rewards card on the market today, and we believe we are responsible credit risks and deserve a chance with your card.

We do not need a large credit limit and would be happy with a small credit line at first to prove to you our reliability. Although I am not including our most recent paystubs or tax returns, I will submit them if requested.

I look forward to your reconsideration and receipt of my new Starwood Preferred Guest Amex card.

Respectfully,

In each example I have made only truthful positive statements about my situation. "Gainfully employed", "Never Been Late on a Payment", "I know my credit score" (you are showing them you care about your credit), and "I only want a small credit line to prove my worth to you."

This has always worked for me, but then again, all the above statements are true. They know it and can see it as well. I think quite a few credit denials are computer generated and when you put your case in front of a human being with these facts, you'll get the card you are after.

Retention Letters

The two questions I am asked most often on my blog are: "Do I have to cancel my previous credit cards before I apply for a new one?" and "When should I cancel my existing credit cards?"

Here are my answers:

You do not have to cancel your existing cards in order to acquire new ones unless credit card lenders report you have too many cards or too high of a limit with the card issuer already. They will let you know in your denial letter. In this case, call them or write them and offer to close one of your old cards so you can get the new one you want. Or, offer to reduce the credit limit on an older card so they can approve your new card application. One word of warning here: *NEVER* cancel your *OLDEST* credit cards. They provide the "aging" to your credit report that shows how long of a successful credit history you have. The length of your successful history is very important to your score.

Don't be in a hurry to cancel your existing credit cards. *Don't pass up this opportunity for more free miles.*

You'll want to ask your credit card company for a *retention bonus* for being a good customer or for agreeing to pay the annual renewal fee.

The annual fee comes at the end of one year using the card. The company will send you a statement with the annual fee on it. If you cancel the card at that time, they will waive the annual fee and the card is cancelled.

The better option is to call the number on the back of your credit card and tell them you are considering cancelling their card (due to the annual fee), or because you want to try a new rewards program. In many cases they will offer you a retention bonus to keep their card. The bonus may be in the form of a bonus of 3,000 to 10,000 miles or points to renew the card. It may be in a waiver of the renewal fee or possibly an increase in your award earning, maybe double points for the next six months, if you keep their card.

This technique is a plain and simple case of:

"If you don't ask, you'll never know."

Once you know their offer, then decide whether to keep the card or cancel it. And you can do this at anytime throughout the year.

My Favorite Credit Card

When I am not meeting the minimum spend requirement for a new credit card, my personal favorite is the Starwood Preferred Guest credit card by American Express. I use it because:

The SPG points earned have the highest value of any single point. (My estimate is 2.5 to 3 cents each)

There is no annual fee the first year, and only a $65 annual renewal fee, thereafter.

The points earned can be converted into airline miles with 30 different airlines and a 5000 mile bonus is applied when transferring in blocks of 20,000.

The "cash and points" option for hotel redemptions provides the highest dollar value for their points and is a great use of SPG points.

Points in different accounts for different family members at the same mailing address can readily be combined.

I use this card every day, day in and day out, wherever American Express is accepted, as do many other miles and points collectors. When the Freddie awards were issued, this card won the Best All Around Travel Card year after year. You'll find an ad for the card application on my blog: Frugaltravelguy.com. I get a small referral if you use my ad.

We have covered much in this section. There is a lot of information to grasp, but the rewards can be huge, if you always keep in mind:

"Your credit is one of your most important assets"

Machu Picchu, Peru

Rental Car Promotions

Rental cars offer an additional source of frequent flyer miles or hotel points that at times can be quite significant.

It seems all the major car rental companies want to affiliate with all the major airlines. There is no exclusivity among the relationships. That is good for us as consumers because they often try to outdo one another with a larger and more lucrative promotion. Here is an example:

If Avis offers 5000 bonus Delta miles with a one-day rental, Budget may retaliate with a 10,000 mile bonus for a two-day rental. Rental car companies never seem to carry the same terms and conditions regardless if the same airline is involved. Possibly their contracts may require distinctions, but they sure fight for the loyalty business within frequent flyer programs. In fact, to partake in many of the mileage promotions you are required to use a specific coupon code and promotion offer code in order to reap the benefits. The company's logic is that loyal Delta flyers already have a Delta-affiliated promo code in their online profiles, and would just continue from force of habit.

Wise rental car shoppers will check out the variety of affiliated rental car offers connected to their favorite airline.

You may decide, in some cases, to actually accumulate frequent flyer miles from a different airline program should the offer be good enough to warrant a switch in loyalty.

Several years ago Budget had a rental car offer that was so good it made sense to rent a car even if you never drove it. If you rented an SUV, premium or luxury car for a one day minimum, entered the proper promotion and coupon codes, you would receive 9,999 Delta airlines miles. The wholesale value of the frequent flyer miles exceeded the cost of the car rental.

As consumers Katy and I would drive to the Hilton Head airport where we could rent an intermediate sized SUV on the weekend for $42 per day. If $42 got me 10,000 miles, my math said that 5 rentals at $42 each or $210 would get me 50,000 miles and a coach class ticket to Europe. Ten rentals or $420 equaled a business class ticket to Europe. We rented cars every weekend day for a whole winter while this promotion went on. We'd drive to the airport, I'd return my rental car and Katy would pick up hers. Rinse and repeat the next day. With Thursday, Friday, Saturday and Sunday available at the lower weekend rate, we were each picking up 20,000 miles per weekend for $84 each.

That may seem like a ton of work for 20,000 miles, but we were only 5 minutes from our tiny little airport with no parking hassles or inconvenience.

Another enterprising young man took a different tack. He rented 14 intermediate SUV's from the Seattle SeaTac airport all on the same day. He filled out the paper work on each rental and never took them off the rental lot. His haul was 14 x 9,999 miles for 14 times the one day price at SeaTac.

The keys to rental car success are watching for the significant promos as a consumer, or if a business traveler, making use of the best promo available for each of your business rentals. There are some benefits to customer loyalty in the rental car business, but some of these promos far overshadow the convenience you get from rental car elite status.

The key here is to keep your eyes open with email alerts, or watch the travel blogs for significant offers. I also like to check a website called CarRentalSavers.com for cash discounts.

There is also a thread on Flyertalk.com in the MilesBuzz forum, started anew each quarter of the year, for example called Car Rental Bonus Promos!. Follow that thread for the latest bonus promotions.

Shotover River
Queenstown, New Zealand

"Expedia.Uk Refer a Friend Promo"

One of the nicest benefits of writing my blog, frugaltravelguy.com, is the number of people that want to partake in the promotions I find. The British Expedia site and my blog readers saved Katy and me over $1000 in 2009 with their Refer a Friend promo.

The promo worked like this: When I referred you to Expedia.co.uk and you signed up for their email offerings, they would send you a £20 voucher which you could use on your next Expedia.uk hotel booking. You were a $30 winner. When you made that booking, Expedia.uk would in turn send me a £40 voucher that we could use on our next hotel booking. The promotion came just in time for us to use for booking 18 nights of hotels in NZ. Using £40 vouchers for 18 hotel stays reduced the cost of our trip $1080!

That promo was a win-win for all concerned. Most of the promotions I recommend will be. My blog usually has an offer for an extra 1000 miles here or a $$ off voucher there if you let me refer you. I try my best to make sure "you" the reader benefit first, and if I get something for referring you, all the better. I find a good number of airline and hotel promotions for new signups. You will receive a benefit for allowing me to refer you, that you would not have received if you did it on your own.

One of the best ongoing referrals I have is for people interested in the Bank Direct Mileage Checking account. With my referral you will pick up an additional 1000 AA miles. I receive an extra 1000 miles as well. One of my readers has earned in excess of 100,000 AA miles as a result of banking with Bank Direct.

Check out that offer and others at
FrugalTravelGuy.com

Online Shopping Portals

I'm not a shopper, except when the deal is right and I'm properly rewarded for buying online. There are some fantastic opportunities to build up your frequent flyer and hotel points accounts if you shop online.

Most airline and hotel website have online shopping malls with affiliated retailers in all categories. I mean every category you can think of. At times there are so many options as to where to best make your online purchase, it becomes confusing. But we have two websites to help us decide which online mall offers the best reward for shopping with them. (Prices being equal of course)

RewardsDB.com and Evrewards.com scour the web everyday looking for the reward offerings from a multitude of online shopping websites. Their investigation includes non-affiliated sites where you may exchange your rewards points for travel items as well as the airline and hotel websites. There are over 95 shopping programs online offering rewards.

If you need a pair of LL Bean cargo pants, go to the RewardsDB.com website, enter the merchant name LL Bean and all the available rewards points options will be prominently displayed for you. It is now your job to compare prices and decide which offers the most value to you.

During your search, keep in mind that non-affiliated website rewards may be exchanged for travel rewards. The site I use most often is Airmilesmart.com which allows me convert Airmilesmart.com award points to Starwood Preferred Guest Rewards hotel points (SPG). This is just one example in millions. Think of rewards as a discount when shopping online through an online mall.

Holiday time is a great time for online shopping; many merchants increase the award points they offer for purchases. During the holidays is not uncommon to be offered double the points. Shipping is also prepaid on many sites for purchases over a certain dollar amount.

Another website I have used is drugstore.com for non perishable household items. I locate drugstore.com in my favorite online shopping mall and order items such as soap, detergent, paper towel, toothpaste etc. for delivery to my home. Again, I'm not a shopper, and I anticipate you will make better use of this rewards opportunity than I do.

Financial Services and Banking

Where you bank can also have a huge influence on your frequent flyer miles balances. The three sources of miles accrual are initial account bonuses, monthly miles earnings for balances held and debit card usage. A fourth source, although very limited, can be a windfall if you happen to find a bank that allows this activity.

New account bonuses are the mainstay of this sector of points earnings. Larger banks and brokerage houses offer an initial sign up bonus based on the size of the initial deposit. Smaller initial balance requirements typically yield lower miles bonuses. The two principal players from the brokerage houses are TD Ameritrade and Fidelity. Lesser players are Sharebuilder and MyStockfund.

TD Ameritrade and Fidelity offer sign-up bonuses of up to 25,000 frequent flyer miles, but require initial deposits of up to $50,000 to achieve that type of award. Sharebuilder and MyStockFund offer sign-up bonuses in the 2000 to 5000 mile range for much smaller initial deposits. Before investing your hard earned cash with these institutions it is important to compare the rate of return earned with these companies to the rates offered by firms that do not deliver miles. If you have a value of the miles you'll earn in mind, the comparison becomes quite simple.

Another important factor is the length of time you leave your funds on deposit.

Banks, typically the national brands, (Citi, US Bank, Chase etc.) will offer sign-up bonuses for opening either a new checking or savings account. It seems there is always a promotion available. Some of the promotions require you, as a new depositor, to set up a direct deposit into the account, pay a bill electronically from the account or use an associated debit card a minimum of times per month. The idea behind these requirements is to accustom you to using the account, hopefully keeping it open after you receive your sign up bonus.

Chase Bank has been one of my favorite banks when looking for sign up bonuses. They seem to have an offer available all the time for a personal checking and a separate bonus available for opening a business checking account. Over the last 4 or 5 years the bonus has been either a cash award or 25,000 Continental Airlines miles for each of the personal and business checking accounts and associated debit cards. Katy and I have each picked up an easy 50,000 miles each year for the last four years with little effort and only a small charge for the debit card.

Suntrust Bank, a regional bank in the southeast offered for a short time 15,000 Delta miles for opening a personal account, allowing you to add two authorized users. Each paid $55 for the debit card and the miles all posted to the original depositor's Delta Skymiles account.

The corresponding business checking account allowed 4 authorized users so we each picked up 5 x 15,000 miles equals 75,000 miles at a cost of $275. Added to the 45,000 miles we accumulated each from the personal account our total haul was 120,000 miles for $440. That's a pretty cheap First Class ticket to Europe, or calculated as domestic tickets, about $150 each.

In regards to the debit cards, additional usage also earns miles for PIN transactions at the rate of typically 1 mile per dollar spent. If you are familiar with using a debit card and getting nothing for loyalty, you may want to consider switching to a miles earning debit card.

One bank I continue to use is Bank Direct located in Texas, the home of American Airlines. Bank Direct has a variation on the typical sign up bonus. They will give you a small miles sign up bonus for opening an account, another bonus for setting up a direct deposit, another for using their bill pay system and one more for referring customers to the bank. Lastly, the best of the bonuses is earning miles for the dollars you have on deposit each month in your checking account. The interest paid by Bank Direct for the Mileage Earning checking account is .05% (virtually nothing) but you earn 100 American Airlines miles for every $1000 you have on deposit, each month. If you calculate the value of 1200 AA miles at 1.5 cents each, your earnings are $18 per year or 1.8%. When you take into account that the earning of miles is typically a non taxable event (check with your tax expert) the yield is pretty good for a checking account. There are no fees for this account if the minimum balance is over $2500.

The fourth source of earnings from banks and brokerage houses is not a typical event, not well publicized, and only available at a very small percentage of institutions. Some institutions will let you make the initial deposit into your new checking or savings account by placing a charge on your credit card and treating that transaction as a purchase, hence a miles earning event.

We have, in the past, funded over $150,000 in new accounts this way. The bank that allowed us to use our credit card to initially fund has now changed their system, but we actually earned 150,000 American Airline miles with this technique. We just left the funds in the new accounts until the credit card bills came due and then paid the credit card bills with the new funds on deposit.

I don't think this size of bonanza still exists but many smaller banks are hungry for new accounts and reports of funding with a credit card (treated as a purchase) still abound online. If you find one in your local area that will let you open an account that way, please drop me an email.

Consumer Promotions

Consumer promotions appear out of the blue sky with no rhyme or reason and can really fill up your frequent flyer account quickly and inexpensively.

As companies struggle to improve their market share or the image of their product, they will try some crazy things to be noticed. Frequent flyer miles given as bonuses catch everybody's eye.

I've related stories about waffles and drink cups, magazines and discount vouchers. There are many more consumer promotions, some that worked well for the company and some that are terrific for the collector. The great promotions are good for both parties.

Other products that have had frequent flyer mile bonuses include Emmi cheese wheels, Dannon water, Healthy Choice pudding cups, and Nutragrain bars. There are many, many more, some running right now I'm sure. My all time favorite and weirdest was the Bosley Hair Restoration Clinic.

In 2008 if you scheduled and attended a free initial consultation at a Bosley Hair Restoration Clinic you were awarded 20,000 Delta Airlines miles. The twenty-minute consultation was professional and painless. Men with full heads of hair, women and children over 18 all took advantage of the offer.

I found out that I was thinning in front (like I didn't know) and it could be resolved in one sitting for a mere $11,000 approximately. And, if I acted now, I would receive an additional 150,000 Delta miles after paying for the treatment.

The gal at the Bosley reception desk said that the endeavor was very successful for their office as they had people arriving for consultations all day, every day during the promotion.

The point to be made here is that you are surrounded by opportunities to travel very well at very reasonable prices if you just keep your eyes open. And if you don't have time to keep current with the latest promos, at least subscribe to a travel blog or two that will watch the market for you.

"Around the World on the US Mint"

In June of 2008 a thread showed up on Flyertalk.com, describing how one could purchase newly minted $1 coins directly from the US Mint and have them shipped to your home or office without a handling charge or shipping. We were off and running.

It seems Congress had mandated the circulation of new coins reflecting deceased US Presidents and historical Native Americans. Congress neglected to remove the paper bills from circulation, and nobody wanted to make the change. The US public has for the most part rejected the $1 coin. Enter "frequent flyer collectors" to the rescue.

We are able to buy these coins directly from the Mint without fees or shipping charges and charge the purchases to our mileage earning credit cards. When the coins arrive, some are spent and put in circulation. Many are taken to local banks and deposited into the checking and savings accounts of the miles and points collectors.

When the credit card bills come due each month a check is written to pay off the credit card with the funds deposited in the form of coins. An almost perfect circle has been formed. The Mint got their coins in circulation, or so they thought, and we loaded up our frequent flyer accounts for no charge, just for the effort of hefting a few thousand coins around (38.65 pounds per 2500 to be exact).

Local banks were at times willing to accept the coins and others were extremely dismayed at the prospect of having coins (their customers did not want) filling up their vaults. Who was going to pay for having all these coins shipped back to the Federal Reserve Banks? Unless the bank had a clearly written policy on charging fees for large coin deposits how could they turn down their customers depositing legal tender? That's what they are in the business to do.

Some took this windfall to an extreme level. One individual reported online that they had purchased over $800,000 in coins. In fact, a Wall Street Journal article appeared after he was interviewed exposing the windfall for points collectors. The US Mint attempted to amend their policies and limit the number of coins ordered per household. They continue changing their policies and the struggle still continues as of this writing. Remember, that the Mint is mandated by Congress to get these coins in circulation. If the banks don't want them, and retail customers don't want them, we, the frequent flyer collectors seem to be their only hope of moving these things into the system.

Since 2008 Katy and I have ordered a few of these coins ourselves. Our Around the World itinerary in 2009 was made possible by this technique. I'd order coins with my Starwood

Preferred Guest card coupled with my normal spending. Once I accumulated 20,000 Starwood points I'd convert them to American Airlines miles.

180,000 American Airlines miles is sufficient to book an Around the World itinerary in Business Class, provided the flight miles total up to no more than 35,000 miles all traveling in the same direction. Katy and I flew from Savannah, Georgia to Lima, Peru and on to Machu Picchu, Iguassu Falls, Argentina and then to Rio de Janeiro. After our time in South America we flew on to Zurich, Switzerland where we traveled by train for three weeks through Switzerland, Austria and Germany. Our next flights took us to Bangkok, Thailand where we added side trips to Siem Reap, Cambodia to wander the Temples of Angkor Wat and to Phuket, Thailand for a week at the Marriott Resort.

From Thailand we continued through Sydney, Australia where we stopped to spend time with my son who is a clinical researcher in a local hospital. We then finished our trip with a week's rest and relaxation in Hawaii before heading home to Hilton Head Island, South Carolina.

The cost of our Around the World Business Class tickets amounted to $316.20 each for taxes and fees. The rest was compliments of the US Mint.

The US Mint program is still mandated through 2013 and coins are still being purchased. I'm sure the Mint will come up with a more efficient way to distribute the coins but for now, they continue to struggle on how to get them into circulation. They are obviously aware of collectors that are benefiting, and they are constantly revising their shipping rules and limits per household. Ingenious collectors have more than one credit card address and more than one shipping address. The cat and mouse game continues.

Conclusion

In summary, I have provided you the means to reduce your travel budget. Whether or not this becomes a hobby, passion, obsession or addiction, you will save money on travel today and for the rest of your life. Follow these simple guidelines and you will be amazed at how the world of travel will open itself up to you with opportunities.

Subscribe by RSS feed or email alert to several travel blogs.

My favorites are:

>   Frugaltravelguy.com by yours truly
>   One Mile at a Time by Ben Schlappig
>   View from the Wing by Gary Leff
>   Loyalty Traveler by Ric Garrido

Join each of the major domestic airline programs and hotel programs. Have each member of your immediately family do so as well. Keep the membership numbers and passwords in a travel folder.

Be aware of fare wars to Hawaii. They happen often and save you hundreds of dollars on tickets to this magical destination. Read the blogs.

Never call the airline or hotel if you suspect you have found a Mistake Fare. Others are trying to book the offer as well.

Don't be greedy. Take only what you will reasonably use.

Practice using Priceline, Biddingfortravel and Tripadvisor techniques on an imaginary trip in the future. *Just don't hit* the "Buy my Hotel" button.

Join the Google group for the Best Rate Guarantee blog and read up on the latest hotel Best Rate Guarantee options.

Volunteer to be *bumped* for every segment of your next airline trip if time will allow.

Write a professional and courteous letter to an airline customer service department the next time something goes awry with your flight or travel plans.

Join the RewardsNetwork Dining program of your favorite airline. Register a credit card with the program and eat out at their member restaurants.

Check your credit report for accuracy and credit score. There are free trial offers listed on frugaltravelguy.com, provided you cancel within the trial period. You are striving for scores over 700 on the FICO scale and 800 on the VantageScore scale.

Review the current promotions for car rentals when you need a rental car. Free miles after all, are *free miles*.

When shopping online, use the research tools of Evrewards.com and RewardsDB.com.

Lastly, and most important, *Keep your Eyes Open*. When you start to think of airline miles and hotel points on a regular basis, in your daily life, and as a normal routine, then you will find yourself with the opportunity to:

See the World at Prices We all Can Afford

34291922R00059

Made in the USA
Lexington, KY
31 July 2014